G000075168

Ar Lan y Môr

Arranged for SATB choir
by
Patrick Hartnett

First published in Great Britain by Springtime Books, 2020

ISBN: 978-1-8381746-2-0

Commissioned by the Mountain Ash & District Choral Society in honour of our President, Phyllis Brace, on her 90th birthday.

Penblwydd Hapus, Miss

Ar Lan y Môr

Geiriau Cymraeg: traddodiadol
Alaw: traddodiadol

Traditional Welsh folk song
Arranged by Patrick Hartnett

Copyright 2020: Patrick Hartnett
First published in Great Britain by Springtime Books, 2020
ALL RIGHTS RESERVED

4

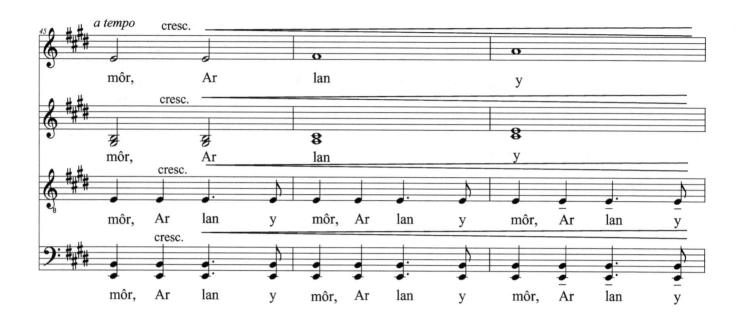

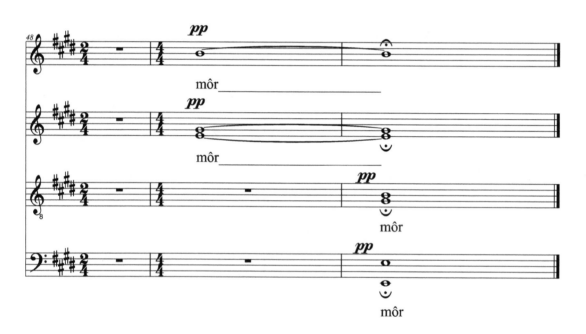

Ar lan y môr mae rhosys cochion

Ar lan y môr mae lilis gwynion

Ar lan y môr mae 'nghariad inne

Yn cysgu'r nos a chodi'r bore.

Beside the sea red roses growing

Beside the sea white lilies showing

Beside the sea their beauty telling

My true love sleeps within her dwelling.

Ar lan y môr mae carreg wastad

Lle bûm yn siarad gair â'm cariad

O amgylch hon fe dyf y lili

Ac ambell gangen o rosmari.

Beside the sea the stones lie scattered

Where tender words in love were uttered

While all around there grew the lily

And sweetest branches of rosemary.

Ar lan y môr mae cerrig gleision

Ar lan y môr mae blodau'r meibion

Ar lan y môr mae pob rinweddau

Ar lan y môr mae nghariad innau.

Beside the sea blue pebbles lying

Beside the sea gold flowers glowing

Beside the sea are all things fairest

Beside the sea is found my dearest.

Arranger's Note

Ar Lan y Môr is a hugely popular Welsh folk song, loved by many. Its gentle melody lends itself well to choral arrangements, and this new version for SATB choir weaves simple, warm harmonies around the haunting tune. The piece ends with a short musical postscript that symbolises love: a repetition of the song's title that grows in intensity until, suddenly, we are left with the gentle stillness of the sea.

Patrick Hartnett
Chedgrave, Norfolk
2020

About the Mountain Ash & District Choral Society

The Mountain Ash & District Choral Society is one of the oldest mixed choirs in South Wales with its roots dating back to 1964. The first rehearsal was in January 1965, at the former Bethlehem Chapel, High St., Mountain Ash under the baton of Phyllis Morley-Jones, with Lyndon Howells as accompanist. As the name suggests, although based in Mountain Ash, it draws its members from as far afield as Cardiff, Merthyr and Glynneath.

www.mountchoral.co.uk